W9-BMU-777

Introduction

In an oral tradition true riddles seem to offer a playful challenge to the people's conventional views of their world. They do this by describing the familiar in words and terms that make it sound magical and mysterious. Unlike other forms of the riddle, true riddles aim not to trick or puzzle but to offer a fresh view of the world. To me they are poems – peoples' poetry.

Pat Fairon
Loughgall, Co. Armagh
1992

Answers
Answers to the riddles are on page 60.

A steel pig going over a bone bridge
and a brass man driving it.

EST.1921 S. EWING & SONS

PHILIP BLUSTINE '92.

PAT FAIRON

IRISH RIDDLES

ILLUSTRATED BY *Philip Blythe*

CHRONICLE BOOKS

SAN FRANCISCO

First published in 1992 by
The Appletree Press
19-21 Alfred Street
Belfast BT2 8DL
Tel: +44 1232 243 074 Fax: +44 1232 246 756
Copyright © 1992 The Appletree Press Ltd.
Printed in the E.U. All rights reserved.
No part of this publication may be reproduced
or transmitted in any form or by any means,
electronic or mechanical, photocopying,
recording or in any information and retrieval
system, without permission in writing
from Chronicle Books.

Irish Riddles

Jacket design by Karen Smidth.

First published in the United States in 1992 by
Chronicle Books, 275 Fifth Street,
San Francisco, CA 94103

ISBN 0-8118-1087-9

9 8 7 6 5 4 3 2 1

Acknowledgements
For permission to reproduce material the following
acknowledgements are made: The Head of the
Department of Irish Folklore, University College
Dublin, for material from Schools Manuscripts; the
Secretary of the Folklore of Ireland Society, Dublin,
for material from the journal *Bealoideas*; and the
County Museum, Armagh, for material from the
Patterson Collection.

It was in the river but wasn't drowned
It was in the grass but wasn't cut
It was in the shop but wasn't sold.

As white as milk but milk it's not
As green as grass but grass it's not
As red as a rose but rose it's not.
As black as ink but ink it's not.

Philip Blythe '92.

Who do I see coming through the sea
But the toy of the sun
A man with a blue coat
And a red thread in his shirt.

Big biddy from the north
Has a big mouth but can't talk
Two iron ears and can't hear
Three iron legs and can't walk.

It once was low
But now it's high
It once was wet
But now it's dry
It once was black
But now it's red
I put it upstanding
And it fell down dead.

Two brothers we are, great burdens
we bear
In which we are bitterly pressed
The truth we do speak, we are full
all the day
And empty when we go to rest.

When I'm old they cut me
And in a hole they put me
When I'm three months old
They come looking me quite bold
Between fire and water they
burn me
Between two irons they turn me
And when I'm stripped of my skin
They find a hole to put me in.

Hidi Hadi on the wall
Hidi Hadi got a fall
Three men and threescore
Wouldn't leave Hidi Hadi
As he was before.

A hopper o' ditches
A cropper o' corn

A wee brown cow
And a pair of leather horns.

Through a rock, through a reel
Through an old spinning wheel
Through a bag of feathers
Through an old mud wall
If that's not a riddle
There's no riddle at all.

Brothers and sisters have I none
But this man's father
Was my father's son.

Who is it?

I washed my face in water
That was never rained or run
I dried it with a towel
That was neither wove nor spun.

Philip Bliss 92

In a marble hall
As white as milk
Lined with a skin
As soft as silk
Within a fountain
Crystal clear
A golden apple doth appear
No doors there are to this
stronghold
Yet thieves break in to steal
the gold.

A bannock of bread
And a sheet full of crumbs.

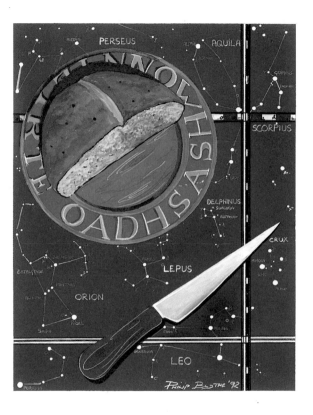

A house full
A room full
And couldn't catch
A spoonful.

Two legs on the ground
And three legs overhead
And the head of the living
In the mouth of the dead.

Neither fish nor flesh
Nor feathers nor bone
But still has fingers
And thumbs of its own.

As I went through yon guttery gap
I met a wee man in gay red cap
A stick in his stern and a stone
in his belly
Riddle me that and I'll give
you a penny.

Hink! Hank! On the bank
Ten drawing four.

A hard-working father
And an easygoing mother
Twelve little children
As black as one another.

As black as ink
As white as milk
And hops on the road
Like hailstone.

As round as an apple
As deep as a pail
She'll never bawl out
Till she's caught by the tail.

Hicky Picky locked the gate
Hicky Picky locked it weel
Hicky Picky locked the gate
Without iron or steel!

Four steady standards
Four diddle diddle danders
Two lookers, two hookers
And a wig-wag.

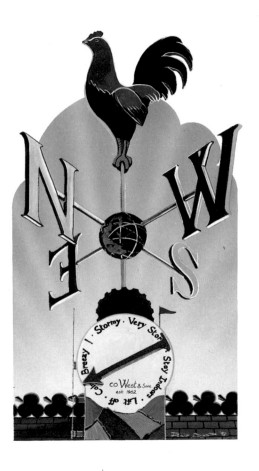

Patch upon patch
Without any stitches
Riddle me that
And I'll buy you some britches.

Long head
Crooked thighs
A wee head
And no eyes!

It ate everything that came
And everything that will
And still it'll never get its fill.

ANSWERS

p.4	A needle and a finger with a thimble
p.7	The sun
p.8	A blackberry
p.11	A rainbow
p.12	A pot
p.15	A sod of turf
p.16	A pair of boots
p.19	A potato
p.20	A broken egg
p.23	A hare
p.24	A moth
p.27	Oneself
p.28	Wash in the dew Dry in the sun
p.31	An egg
p.32	The moon and the stars
p.35	Smoke
p.36	A man with his head in a pot
p.39	A glove
p.40	A haw
p.43	A man milking a cow
p.44	A clock face
p.47	A magpie
p.48	A bell
p.51	Frost
p.52	A cow
p.55	A cabbage
p.56	The tongs
p.59	A graveyard